THE ATTITUDE BOOK

50 WAYS TO POSITIVELY AFFECT YOUR LIFE AND WORK

SIMON TYLER

PRAISE FOR
THE ATTITUDE BOOK

Published by
LID Publishing Limited
The Record Hall, Studio 204,
16-16a Baldwins Gardens,
London EC1N 7RJ, UK

524 Broadway, 11th Floor, Suite 08-120,
New York, NY 10012, US

info@lidpublishing.com
www.lidpublishing.com

A member of:

www.businesspublishersroundtable.com

© Simon Tyler, 2018
© LID Publishing Limited, 2018

Printed in Latvia by Jelgavas Tipogrāfij

ISBN: 978-1-910649-88-6

Cover and page design: Caroline Li and Matthew Renaudin

THE
ATTITUDE
BOOK

50 WAYS TO POSITIVELY AFFECT
YOUR LIFE AND WORK

SIMON TYLER

LONDON   NEW YORK   BOGOTA
MADRID   BARCELONA   BUENOS AIRES
MEXICO CITY   MONTERREY   SAN FRANCISCO
SHANGHAI

FOR OTHER TITLES IN THE SERIES...

CONCISE
ADVICE
LAB

SMALL BOOKS: BIG IDEAS

CLEVER CONTENT, DYNAMIC IDEAS, PRACTICAL
SOLUTIONS AND ENGAGING VISUALS –
A CATALYST TO INSPIRE NEW WAYS OF THINKING
AND PROBLEM-SOLVING IN A COMPLEX WORLD

conciseadvicelab.com

CONTENTS

ACKNOWLEDGMENTS

The more I worked on the content for *The Attitude Book*, the more immersed I became in noticing the power of attitude and how it works every day.

I would like to thank those who have patiently listened, advised and added to my thinking on this particular journey, irrespective of whether they realised they were actually helping me!

Most particularly, I would like to acknowledge Simon Emmett, Sara Taheri and the team at LID Publishing, my clients and, of course, my friends and family.

INTRODUCTION

Dictionary definitions of attitude broadly capture three variants of what attitude is; your manner, mood, disposition or feeling regarding another person, situation or thing; your corresponding posture or body position to express the mind's choices; and the third is from aeronautics – which describes an aircraft's attitude as the inclination of it's three principal axes, relative to the wind and the ground.

I like all three and notice that they are almost one and the same.

The aeronautics definition is a useful metaphor that brings together everything that I have discovered in my work on attitude, it being how our three axes (body, thought and mind) are inclined to the conditions we face.

The convergence of these definitions, and my observations and dis-coveries, have led me to a definition of attitude as:

The choice, conscious or unconscious, to hold yourself in thought, mind and body in relation to anything that shows up.

For most people, it is about letting circumstances influence and set their attitude – in which case we get hurled around by the winds of our life and imminent impact with the ground of reality!

It's not about choosing an extreme euphoric stance irrespective of your current situation – sometimes turbulent conditions require an adapted inclination or attitude.

It is about choosing the attitude based on conditions, your destination and the desire for a smooth flight and landing (every time!).

This book is your transit guide as you bring to the surface every single component of your attitude set-up, trial new methods and develop your capability to do some incredible things with just the power of your attitude.

THE SHIFTED ATTITUDE

One of my favourite Wayne Dyer phrases is: *"If you change the way you look at things, the things you look at change."* This means that the attitude you are wearing at any moment pre-determines how you experience everything that's going on.

We live in a time where problems seem to proliferate around the world, all the time. They are frequently reported, feasted upon and given massive air time. We are experiencing a global obsession with complexities and bad news. Seven billion attitudes are at risk!

Happy (your own upgraded version of it) is the ultimate attitude.

Clues that you'll know when your attitude has shifted:

a) Your heart is happy (from its calmness, to its beat and its warmth).
b) You smile more often.
c) The feelings you experience are enjoyable.

HOW TO USE THIS BOOK

The chapters in *The Attitude Book* are named **Attitude Shifters**. When contemplated, experimented and acted upon, each Attitude Shifter will halt 'sub-optimal attitudes', find and establish attitude middle-ground and inspire you to raise your attitude to a higher, more powerful positive place.

In working with each **Attitude Shifter** you will either reselect, protect or boost your attitude.

These **Attitude Shifters** are designed as stand-alone inspirers – you can dip in and out of *The Attitude Book*, or read entire sections at a time. You do not need to read them in the sequence I have laid out here in order to achieve maximum benefit.

Try to change something in your routine, week by week. Introduce one idea at a time in order to fully absorb the shift in thought and practice.

If you can use just some of the thinking and ideas contained in *The Attitude Book*, you will experience real change. If you work with all **50 Attitude Shifters**, your life path will transform and you will be taking deliberate steps to create new outcomes, new situations and new results. Prepare to astound yourself!

YOUR ATTITUDE RANGE

We have had attitudes since we were tiny babies and life experiences have added, subtracted and refined a set of attitudes that have now become so familiar we hardly think about them.

Your attitude range is your comfort zone, up and down which you travel, from your best days through to your most challenging days. You may get more from this book if at first you consider what your range is – that is, you at your best and you at your worst.

My bad day
attitude

My great day
attitude

Once you have described those two extremes, have a go at defining three points in between to give yourself an escalating attitude scale.

Success with *The Attitude Book* is in shifting your range upward (on both the extreme points) and slowing down the travel through your range.

ATTITUDE IS A CHOICE
YOU JUST KEEP CHOOSING.

ATTITUDE
SHIFTERS

1.
BREATHE

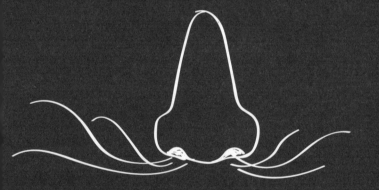

The attitude you have chosen to have right now may not necessarily be the most optimal for the situation you are in, or about to go into, or that you wish to change.

The business of today's life, the pace at which words and moods alter and impact us, means that, before you know it, your attitude is off.

Attitude choice comes from your calm center.

Breathing is the body's natural task, conscious breathing injects a gap, a moment to become calm and get back to overview rather than overwhelm.

a) Pause.
b) Sit or stand comfortably away from distractions.
c) Breathe in slowly through your nose.
d) Hold your breath for a few seconds.
e) Breathe out, slowly and fully.
f) Repeat up to 10 times.

Getting to the 10th repetition will be a challenge at first, as your busy mind attempts to haul you back to thinking about what it considers to be urgent. Persist!

Your attitude will already have shifted and your ability to choose what it will now become has returned.

2.
LOOK WHO'S TALKING

We interact with different people every day. In person, by messaging apps, via audio and video, or through the media.

Every one of those people has an attitude and we are tuning-in to each of their attitudes. The nature of our connection to the other person and the porousness of our attitude determines how much our mood becomes affected or infected by them.

The likelihood is that we pick up a bit of attitude from every one of the people we interact with across a day. Without thoughtful filtration, our attitude becomes a blend of what we held originally and the volume and consistency of those with whom we have interacted.

Whatever the mixture, our attitude may have become ... not ours!

The next time you notice your attitude is, in some way, awry, consider who you have been talking to or listening to that day. What attitudes have you met? How does your current attitude match up with all that?

No surprise there then.

Becoming aware of the affect others have on your attitude is enough, at this stage, to help you become more deliberate and resilient with your own.

● ● ●

• • •

This Attitude Shifter does not apply on those occasions when you are feeling attitudinally strong (you have chosen your attitude and you feel resilient). This applies when you are in the midst of a tough time or working through challenging stuff. On those occasions:

a) Prepare attitude boosters for use before and after your various interactions.
b) Note who you MUST meet/tune into – monitor the effect.
c) Choose to meet/tune into your attitude booster connections – deliberately put time in with those who positively affect your mood and attitude.

THE LIKELIHOOD IS THAT WE PICK UP
A BIT OF ATTITUDE FROM EVERY ONE
OF THE PEOPLE WE INTERACT
WITH ACROSS A DAY.

3.
MOVE

Getting stuck mentally and emotionally is almost always accompanied with a mirrored physical response. We stop moving.

It seems we have this poor inner advisor that says, "Let's just stop, curl up and think our way through this." This doesn't work!

As Albert Einstein famously said:

"We can't solve problems by using the same kind of thinking we used when we created them."

When our attitude has found itself at the grumpy, anxious or miserable end of the range, it's time to move:

a) Get up and stretch.
b) Go for a walk (or run or cycle), ideally for 10 minutes or more, preferably outside.
c) Return, sit, breathe and begin again.

Your attitude selector will have been jolted and choice options will return.

4.
FLOWING
WATER

Experiencing flowing water neutralizes bad attitudes!

I assert this because:
- The human body is 75% water.
- The planet we inhabit is 70% water.
- Harvard physician Cynthia Dorsey, Ph.D., found that 30-minute steam baths taken 1.5 to 2 hours before bedtime improved sleep efficiency in female insomniacs by approximately 10%.
- Flowing water's soothing sounds have long been associated with meditation. Michael Wenger, Dean of Buddhist Studies at the San Francisco Zen Center, describes moving water as 'white noise,' in which you can hear many things.
- The European Centre of Environment and Human Health found that scenes containing water are associated with higher perceived restorativeness than those without water (people are drawn to the colour blue).

This is so simple and abundant as an attitude shifter, it would be churlish to ignore it!

a) Find flowing water. Either actually find it or search for audio recordings and vivid water imagery if you are stuck indoors.
b) Tune in for three minutes, you don't need to think or do anything else.
c) Relax and notice your attitude calm.

Your attitude will already have shifted and your ability to choose what it will now become will flow again.

5.
GRATITUDE

The attitude of gratitude is often quoted as a morally and ethically ideal way to be. When gratitude is absent from our current state, it seems out of reach and the opposite (the grizzly, grumbly version) is in its place.

Gratitude is the act of being thankful, the attitudinal form of this is when you are noticing and being thankful semi-automatically.

Gratitude can:
- Enhance relationships, emotions, health, personality and career.
- Generate social capital faster than negativity – it makes us more likeable.
- Reduce our need for and reliance on materialism.
- Make us less self-centered (or even self-obsessed).
- Increase self-esteem.

The initial effort, to embed this attitude over a few days, is always worth it. Keep it simple:

a) Three times a day (you decide the recurring times), scan your world for three things for which you are grateful.
b) Write them down.
c) Repeat, finding new items each time.

After a few days, your brain's Reticular Activating Cortex, in effect your radar scanner, will have got the message and will begin to do the searching for you.

6.
READ ME

Your brilliant mind is taking in information from a variety of sources all the time.

This attitude shifter is focused on the written word, the articles and notes that you actively and passively consume through your day.

Every note we read speaks to us beyond the actual words used. We may even personify and put a voice to the text if we are in some way connected to the writer, adding an extra layer of interpretation and meaning.

From the instant message or acronym loaded sentence, to the online news article or advertising billboards we pass, each message is communicating to us and encouraging us to think and feel something new.

When you are carrying an uncertain attitude or you are feeling susceptible to outside influences, your attitude is being offered to the metaphorical highest bidder. Let's hope it is a positive winner!

Become more determined:

a) Notice what you are reading and the text you are consuming over the next week.
b) Distill the attitude reaction each is provoking in you.
c) Delete or minimize your exposure to the harmful stuff.
d) Increase or add in positive reading material to balance and boost your attitude.

You will feel the obvious difference.

7.
OUTRAGEOUS
ACTS OF
KINDNESS

Random acts of kindness have often been recognized as spreading good vibes and changing the mood and feeling in the environments within which the act took place. Most notably where the opposite feelings may have prevailed.

Over my years as a coach, with individuals and teams, I have observed the power of such acts and taken the technique to another level, witnessing the positive affect on the attitudes in those involved.

Outrageous Acts of Kindness (**OAK**):

a) Go beyond what would be helpful (let many into a queue of traffic, finish another's uncompleted task, give a gift) – ANONYMOUSLY.
b) Move on, letting go of the action you just took.
c) Repeat (three-a-week?).

Initially, you may feel empty and wish someone had noticed and acknowledged your act. After a few days, you will begin to experience the serotonin sparking, euphoric positive kick from planting seeds of OAK.

8.
THE SILENT
SABOTEUR

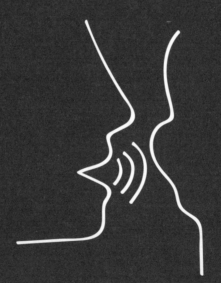

Quietly, in the unspoken, unworded recesses of your mind, lurks a not so dormant feeling, a sensation or a not yet articulated voice that has been delivering unhelpful propaganda messages to your conscious mind.

Like a scurrilous media campaign set on eroding a brand or a person, this inner, almost undetectable voice goes to work to shift attitudes.

When you are at the top or even the middle of your game and enjoying success, you tune in to and receive the positive feedback sent your way and the reward is further determination, confidence and self-belief.

But on those occasions when you are not 'on your game'– generally experiencing self-doubt – propaganda messages from your Silent Saboteur are heard above the rest.

And the messages are familiar and easy to start believing. Your Silent Saboteur has been transmitting in this way for years. You may succumb to the Saboteur's campaign and begin to behave and act consistently with those messages.

Surely now is the time to take action and rid yourself of this Silent Saboteur and begin redirecting its cunning communication channels to more helpful strategies?

● ● ●

• • •

When your demeanour has shifted and your attitude is drifting:

a) Pause, relax, sit calmly and write down (or tell a colleague) what those Silent Saboteur statements might be.
b) Consider each again and notice, honestly, if it was actually true (loosening your mind's grip on the presumed truth).
c) Flip the statements around a few times and explore the new truth of each flip and the different feelings and subsequent thoughts that they ignited.
d) Write out your new 'truths' clearly and often – in notebooks, phones, screens, easy-to-find places. Be ready to switch to them when the last few Silent Saboteur campaigns are being transmitted.

While this may seem an obvious thing to do, the Silent Saboteur's messages become so engrained and silently pervasive that people don't ever take such clearing action steps.

NOW IS THE TIME TO TAKE ACTION
AND RID YOURSELF OF THIS
SILENT SABOTEUR.

9.
SMELL THE ROSES

One of my favourite and much recited phrases is: *"Nothing changes unless something changes,"* and I get it to apply it to many personal development situations!

Many people are stuck, trapped in repeating patterns that simply don't feel great, and the outcomes and results are less than they hoped or just don't give any positive feeling when achieved.

One of the first places they need to focus on is their physical environment. Where are they working, what is their proximity to others, what are the habits and movements of the team (where do they go, repeatedly?).

There is a correlation between that stuck and sometimes glum attitude and the lack of movement and stale or unnaturalness of a working environment.

To sit at a desk in an office, staring at the same things, hoping that the mind switches gears (and attitudes) is futile.

Get Up and Smell the Roses.

Install plants, go out into nature, even for just a few minutes. The dramatic environmental switch will shift your mood and your view on the challenge in which you were once sat will shift.

10.
PLAYLIST

Throughout your life you may well have tuned into various songs and melodies that represent or remind you of an event or an emotionally significant era. These tracks, when heard again, will evocatively take you back to an almost identical emotional memory; who you were with; what you were doing; what you were feeling and thinking.

For the most significant soundtrack memories, you may even notice your entire mind and body state altering to realign with that memory state.

It is a given then that music, sometimes just a few bars and notes, can shift or bolster your mood and attitude, inspiring thoughts and feelings deep inside.

To inspire him through his university thesis creation and exam revision, my son used Ennio Morricone's *Ecstasy of Gold* from the film soundtrack of *The Good, The Bad and The Ugly*. He found it to reliably boost his confidence and sense of certainty.

He played the track recently, almost a year after finishing his course, and I observed how he became fired up again!

● ● ●

● ● ●

Creating your own Attitude Shifter Playlist is a no-brainer, but notice that you may be drawn to listen to music that matches your falling attitude and, in doing so, your attitude embeds or falls further. Instead:

a) Open a playlist folder in your music library and copy in tracks that you find or you can recall have had a positive effect on your mood. Collect, collect, collect.

b) Attribute three attitudes to each – in terms of what they inspire, file them in uniquely named Attitude Shifting Playlists.

c) Listen when you need to ignite your chosen attitude.

THESE TRACKS, WHEN HEARD AGAIN,
WILL EVOCATIVELY TAKE YOU
BACK TO AN ALMOST IDENTICAL
EMOTIONAL MEMORY.

11.
LET IT GO!

The song from Disney's blockbuster animated film *Frozen* has, to a degree, usurped this powerful motivational phrase, so you'll need to get past that to work with this Attitude Shifter.

We all carry a range of stuff inside ourselves; memories; regrets; hopes lost; dreams unfulfilled; incompletes. Our emotional connection to each of them influences our attitude and mood.

In *The 'Keep It Simple' Book,* I wrote about a few releasing techniques to liberate the heaviness of these things (e.g. 'Tolerations', 'Control-Alt-Delete' and 'Your Own CIA').

Releasing some of the deeper and older items in our mental cupboards takes focus and significant work. In this Attitude Shifter, I bring your attention to the 'in the moment' bumps, pot-holes and annoyances that show up and dent, alter or derail our attitude.

They could be a work-stalling power-cut; a PC crash; a traffic jam; a broken cup; an 'urgent' interruption.

The ability to rapidly let go of these irritations is crucial for our attitude health and sustained personal impact.

● ● ●

• • •

When an irritation arrives:

a) **Let it go!** Do nothing with it, breathe and notice your immediate reaction (anger?).
b) **Let it go!** Do nothing with your reaction, breathe slowly and deeply, allowing your brain to cycle through to its next reaction (frustration?).
c) **Let it go!** Do nothing with it, breathe slowly and deeply and choose your response (acceptance, curiosity, willingness to change – whatever feels authentic to you). Articulate it, do something with it and move on.

You can try to turn this into a two-step release but you may find that you have reactions bursting forward that need to be noticed and let go of first.

Your next thoughts, words and actions come from the reaction you grab after the irritation. The letting-go steps mean they come from a better place.

THE ABILITY TO RAPIDLY LET GO OF
THESE IRRITATIONS IS CRUCIAL
FOR OUR ATTITUDE HEALTH AND
SUSTAINED PERSONAL IMPACT.

12.
HOW MUCH
DO YOU 'NO'?

The word 'No' in all languages has deep and evocative meanings, and triggers a range of responses linked to our associations to it in the past and how we use it today. I notice that 'No' is peerless in its ability to assert power over mood and subsequent attitudes.

When you were very young, 'No' was likely to have been the boundary and preventer, the scalder or the shamer. As you grew up, it became the line beyond which it would be deemed wrong to pass. I'm sure it won't take long to tune-in to moments from your past and hear again your 'No' memories.

While working with a client team, I noticed the frequent use of 'No' by a couple of team members in a dialogue. I turned my awareness specifically to the process that followed. Each time 'No' was voiced, even in its most innocent use, there was a palpable and often physically obvious response with the listeners.

Much of its use in language is so casual and habitual, "Oh no"; "No way"; "No, no, I meant this..."; but the impact, particularly the accumulated impact, remains the same.

For the next few hours, or when attending future meetings, listen out for 'No' and notice the reactions.

● ● ●

● ● ●

Putting aside any deeper psychological or emotional reactions, the physical and verbal 'No' responses range from:

- Facial disappointment / varying displays of 'crest-fallen'
- A combative reply
- Resistance
- Stubbornness
- Stiffening of body position
- Detachment (from the subject or the person)
- Disconnection

Perhaps unbeknown to you, you are causing responses that are unhelpful in relationships, slowing down or hindering progress and flow, causing schisms in teams. Repeated use may even be distancing you and your chosen attitude from having the impact it could.

Notice 'No' in use by others, then in your own dialogues, and begin working on reducing its occurrence and shifting to a better option... Saying No Nicely!

EACH TIME 'NO' WAS VOICED, EVEN IN
ITS MOST INNOCENT USE, THERE WAS
A PALPABLE AND OFTEN PHYSICALLY
OBVIOUS RESPONSE WITH
THE LISTENERS.

13.
SAYING NO
NICELY

How is your current workload? Does the inflow seem unrelenting and faster than the outflow? When it comes down to it, might you be involved in too many things or responsible for too much? When you are busy, your attitude gets fogged-up and lost in the melee of activity.

Being the specialist or the reliable one, the 'go-to' person, is a heavy honour. I can still hear former bosses advising me: *"If you want something done, give it to the busy person!"*

While it can be brilliant for your personal brand and notoriety, I have noticed it simply does not correlate with career progress or lead to success. If anything, it can lead to the opposite of your desires – stagnation and the stressful sense of being overwhelmed.

This anathema is confusing, particularly when your automatic response to extreme workload is 'do more, faster', leaving even fewer mindful-moments to rethink your situation.

Simply saying 'No' to the next request may not sit well. What will they think of me? Will this work against me? Would I be missing out? How will the project progress without my magic?

It may be time to develop the attitude shifting skill of 'saying no, nicely'.

● ● ●

● ● ●

a) Before you say 'Yes', invite the requester to "tell me more about...". Enquire about the project. What stage is it at? What are they really asking? What do they specifically want? Who else could help? What exactly needs to be done?

b) Wait, listen and ask another question. Let the other person unravel and broaden their request. I have found that the outcomes of 'saying no nicely' are:

- It gives you more time to contemplate your involvement.
- They elaborate more, meaning you both develop a better solution.
- Another resource can come to mind.
- They end up changing the urgency or the nature of the request.
- They take it back themselves.

c) If you end up taking on this new piece of work, it is taken on with more rigor than your previous habitual response. And it starts to change the expectation that you are an instant yes-er. Your brand elevates one notch!

Your attitude will be shielded or even boosted as you reconnect to the demands placed upon you.

SIMPLY SAYING 'NO' TO
THE NEXT REQUEST
MAY NOT SIT WELL.

14.
REALITY CHECK

Your reality (how it feels to be you, with all your pressures, joys, successes, tensions) feels absolutely real. And, without giving it any conscious thought, it seems it simply is what it is – real, no options. It just is.

To change your reality (and you can) you need to be ready to go against it and defy it! And, as it is almost always your attitude that attracts and confirms your reality, a shift is needed.

Let me illustrate.

For a few weeks, I carried an attitude of "I've got loads to do and little time" plus a bit of "I don't know where to start" with a dash of "I'm not actually getting anywhere". This is a potent mix that left me feeling tense and, at times, anxious and chippy (reacting impatiently with loved ones). I would wear this attitude in facial expressions too and this was obvious to my co-workers.

Put these together and the 'reality' in your home and work situation will be tense, frantic and rushed. You may be achieving a lot, but it doesn't always feel like fun on the way.

This calls for a REALITY CHECK.

a) Explore a way to defy your current reality, to the extent that you still believe in it. i.e. you could trial opposite attitudes.
b) Find three proofs that the alternate reality is already true, tenuous, perhaps, but believable.
c) Keep thinking about it for 30 seconds.

And feel your attitude shifting.

15.
AWESOME
SHORT CUT

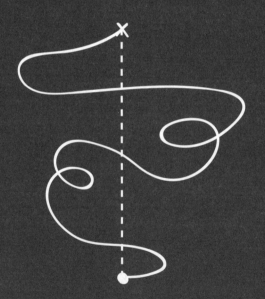

"To sprint through life, without a care
And miss the awesome that's already there."

An incredibly simple yet wise poem – by me.

The attitude of those who are already living an awesome life is dramatically and obviously different from those who are not yet or far from living that awesome life. Which came first, the attitude or the awesome?

That awesome life experience of yours ... is already here. All the components of your great life are knocking around, possibly randomly and haphazardly, but nonetheless nearby, right in your physical and/or metaphysical grasp.

In the inspirational world of positive thinking and motivation, this kind of statement is often made and is challenging to fully believe depending on your current life circumstance. Sometimes it serves only to remind you that it's still not true for you yet. Accept it lightly for a few hours and see if it can take a firmer hold.

It was eating my bacon sandwich one morning that sparked the thinking for this attitude shifter.

Typically, I overloaded my toasted bread with bacon, tomato, mushroom and ketchup (please don't judge me). As if for the first time, I noticed the taste of each individual component separately. I slowed down my habitual rapid munch and turned up my awareness of the crunch of the toast, the slightly earthy squish

● ● ●

● ● ●

of the tomato, the saltiness of the bacon, the buttery-ness of the mushrooms and the piquant vinegary-ness of the ketchup. It didn't markedly change my enjoyment of any particular ingredient, I just noticed them and appreciated them. The sandwich was good!

That's the short-cut. Every now and then, slow things down ever so slightly and notice what's going on – the ingredients. You don't have to like each item any more than you currently do, just notice and appreciate them for what they are. This changes everything.

At your next meeting turn up your awareness and notice the people in the room; the effort; the concentration; the distractions; the resources; the options; the facilities; the pressure.

When you return to your desk, notice the clear spaces; the piles of paper; the sticky notes; the IT kit; the dust; the view; the to do list; the stationery.

You are in the middle of your incredibly abundant life, a potentially awesome experience ... you simply need to notice. In doing so, you will shift your attitude to awesome components previously scattered all around you.

And may your sandwich be good.

THAT AWESOME LIFE
EXPERIENCE OF YOURS...
IS ALREADY HERE.

16.
WORK THE
RESISTANCE

Having gathered dust and a special place in my garden shed for a long while, my bike saw the light of day again recently.

My state of fitness and the local topographic inclines, unnoticed when travelling by car, meant I needed every one of my 21 gears to maintain forward motion. I berated myself as I struggled up the easiest of hills, forcing myself to stay with whatever gear it was and fight my way through the pain, thinking the alternative to be weakness or defeat.

I got through it and, in fact, as you would expect, I noticed how this cycling experience could be a helpful attitude-shifting metaphor.

You and I are not single-geared vehicles. You may not want the image, but you are a refined, multi-geared, super-flexible, multi-paced human. But perhaps, like me on my first bike trips, you may be fighting the resistance, not using your full gear range and becoming drained or even defeated too soon.

Instead you could Work the Resistance!

When your attitude is challenged – as the situation you face becomes complex, difficult in some way, out of your skill set – change down the gears. Doing so is not weakness or defeat. It is finding the resistance and working with it.

• • •

● ● ●

Be honest and mindful; tune in to yourself; get to know how you are feeling in relation to your present situation more accurately and experience your resistance levels throughout the day. Respond accordingly.

Gear down (reduce the resistance) when:
You feel drained; you need more information; your mood has shifted downward; you're with people 'not on the same page'; you experience push-back on your ideas.

Gear up (increase the resistance) when:
It feels easy; you are up for more; your team is thriving; you feel good; your audience is tuned-in.

You will learn fast, it will get easier and more effortless, almost attitude-resistance free living (but we know resistance is always there). Brilliant-cycling you!

WHEN YOUR ATTITUDE
IS CHALLENGED - AS THE
SITUATION YOU FACE
BECOMES COMPLEX -
CHANGE DOWN THE GEARS.

17.
ENOUGH

I am deeply curious about the word 'enough'. It is deceptively ambig-uous and non-specific, yet one of its common uses is in attempting to be specific, in calling for something to end ("That's enough").

This loose use of 'enough' spoils our attitude and leaves us prone to attitude-slippage.

In my work with clients (and with myself!), I observe this word often, paying particular attention to the thoughts and feelings it unconsciously provokes. It nags away in our inner chatter, caus-ing nothing but dissatisfaction, discomfort and the ceaseless demands on what to do. Even "That's enough" never seems to finalize in the way we wish.

Am I enough? Have I done enough? Is that enough time? And so on. All these nebulous and vaguely answerable questions spread like weeds around the garden of our thoughts, making room only for enough's equally insatiable sibling; 'more'!

When left unnoticed, 'enoughing' causes stress, anxiety, tension, impairs attitudes and reduces moment-to-moment happiness. Someone enoughing is prevented from noticing opportunities to kick-back, smile, laugh, chill out, take-stock and generally feel good. It also means that if we decide to push on, i.e. not enough yet, we move further into a deeply dissatisfying space.

● ● ●

● ● ●

I challenge you to notice the use of the word 'enough' in the week ahead, both in your language and in that of colleagues. After it is spoken you will almost immediately notice a drop in mood, a scent of defeat and futility. Inspiration and positive attitudes will leave the room when the 'enough' bell chimes!

a) Just noticing the word will alert you and heighten your greater gifts of articulation. Choose an alternate phrase, be specific, bring your attention and conversation into the now ... what do we have now, what are our options, what appetite, what energy, what focus do we have?
b) Your quality questions (to colleagues and yourself), like throwing ropes, will give you the means to climb up and out of even the toughest situations.
c) Unless of course, you actually HAVE had enough, in which case, get coached and do something about creating and moving to the change you seek.

Enough already!

WHEN LEFT UNNOTICED,
'ENOUGHING' CAUSES STRESS,
ANXIETY, TENSION, IMPAIRS
ATTITUDES AND REDUCES
MOMENT-TO-MOMENT HAPPINESS.

18.
CREATIVE
PROTECTION

When demands for you to create and produce are high, particularly when coupled with your own high expectations, it will overwhelmingly seem that every moment is loaded with a need for you to be doing something productive.

The tighter this tension grips, the less productive you will become!

This type of overwhelm eventually shifts your mood and triggers less than helpful new thoughts. Your attitude is in peril.

A gentle, mindful intervention is required.

I have written about alleviating these tensions and pressures in *The Impact Book* and *The 'Keep It Simple' Book*. Here are three shifters specifically for your attitude that scale up, depending on your state.

a) **Remind Yourself** – that 'everything is ok'. Returning to this simple mantra to trigger memories of times equally or more challenging that you have worked through. Sometimes this is enough of an attitude reset. What is your core reminder statement? Does it need an upgrade?
b) **Mindful Awareness** – any step you take towards mindfulness has a calming and positive effect. All there is to do is notice. How do you feel? What are you thinking? You don't need to change these, just notice them, judgment-free, curious-full. Emotions move (they are in motion). What are your thoughts, feelings and sensations now?

• • •

● ● ●

c) **Meditate** – It may take effort to get yourself to stop and sit quietly so, if your meditation muscle is weak, turn to inspirational music. I have explored widely and experimented often with guided and non-guided meditation tracks, short and long, with and without music or nature sounds or binaural beats. Are you ready to sit quietly? What's on your playlist or what could be to help you?

Enjoy protecting and releasing your creative productivity!

REMIND YOURSELF.
MINDFUL AWARENESS.
MEDITATE.

19.
ROOMITUDE

Yes, it's another word I have brought into the world!

In my observation, 'Roomitude' is the average and pervading attitude in a room of more than three people. It is palpable, not always easy to articulate, but it is there. Extremes are very obvious, particularly when the majority of participants in a room share a common emotion; immense joy and humour, shared sadness and loss.

On arrival in a room setting, your attitude meets with the prevailing roomitude and balances either side of it.

The attitude in most rooms tends to be middling/non-plussed, based on the fact that it contains people with at least one main thing in common (otherwise why would they be there?). Thus, unbeknown to you, your attitude is drawn in toward that average.

It is difficult to sustain a contradictory attitude for long – even if you are full of beans or full of woe. The room will infect and overpower you.

So, you have a choice:

a) Notice yours.
b) Notice theirs (both the roomitude and the attitudes of those in your immediate proximity).
c) Then either:
   • Detect and move toward those matching your attitude.
   • Go with those who need you most (you will upgrade the roomitude most markedly there).

'Attitude Up' is the goal here. Use your environment to support, sustain and uplift your prevailing attitude.

20.
QUESTION
YOURSELF

"The answers you seek,
Are in the questions you speak."

Another incredibly wise poem – by me.

Change, to any situation or attitude, comes as a result of circumstances or choice. To provoke the more determined and deliberate change, we cannot leave it to chance.

Moments of clarity, insights, light bulb flashes, inspiration, waves of impetus, come when:

a) You are feeling good in some way, when your outlook and attitude is positive, when you are in environments that uplift you, when you are with people that ignite you.
b) You work through brilliant questions, asked of you or by you.

When you are not in those inspiring situations, you can still experience breakthrough attitude shifts but it will not come automatically. That level of thinking comes only from the questions you hold yourself to answer.

When your mood is suboptimal, your corresponding range of questions may be not much better than 'why am I doing this?' (personal blame) or 'why is this happening' (external blame). You could get stuck in blaming, complaining or justifying your current circumstance.

● ● ●

a) Take two or three days tuning in to your own questions. What are you asking yourself? The range of answers and the impact they have on your thoughts thereafter are totally aligned to the mood and emphasis of what you are asking.

b) Next, carry a couple of the following questions (no more than three!) with you and substitute them. Let them percolate into your thinking and notice how your range of answers improve, feel better and provoke more uplifting follow-on thinking.

c) As you practice this (and it does take practice, don't give up too soon), find your own questions that provoke the mood and thinking you desire and add them to your list. Keep them simple, short and artfully vague (and that's a coaching secret!).

Ask great questions of others too and watch their attitudes improve.

WHAT DO I REALLY WANT?
WHAT IS POSSIBLE NOW?
HOW COULD I USE THIS?
WHAT DO I WANT NOW?
WHAT DO I WANT MORE OF?
WHAT DO I ENJOY MOST?
WHAT DO I FIND EASY?
WHERE WAS I AT MY BEST?
WHAT ELSE MIGHT BE HAPPENING HERE?
WHO ELSE HAS EXPERIENCED THIS?
WHAT DO I REALLY THINK ABOUT THIS?
WHAT DOES THIS TEACH ME?

21.
INTEGRITUDE

High integrity lies at the heart of powerful and effective attitudes, thus my elevation of the concept to Integritude! Integrity can be the one thing that anchors your attitude and holds you in place.

The volume and potency of commercial perils that surround us today (low trust, fake news, scamming and acts of low business integrity) have created an expectation that they are now expected, and, dangerously, accepted parts of our working lives.

For a long while now, I have been harangued by PPI (Payment Protection Insurance) refund-hunters, pension sorters, must-buy-now dealers and have become battle-hardened to withstand the onslaught of calls, emails and letters. On reflection, I noticed the impact of low-integrity activities; they breed; they make more of such acts acceptable; scepticism is rife. I am utterly convinced it isn't, nor ever could be, an environment in which we can thrive, grow, be inspired, create great moments, achieve wonderful things or feel complete. Again I note; attitudes are in peril!

The response choices you and I face are:

a) **Retaliate** – this is flawed and perpetuates, or even justifies, the awfulness.
b) **Rampage, campaign, complain** – likely to be futile, misinterpreted and hugely demanding on energy.
c) **Rise Up** – enhance your own integrity – change has to start somewhere.

● ● ●

• • •

A while back I was with my son, who at the time of this story was nine years old. We were in a shop and he chose and bought a sticky-sweet but, as we left the shop, he realized the shop assistant had charged us incorrectly. He briefly held a cheeky false-victory grin. We talked about it and decided to go back and pay the additional 20p. My son felt good, the two staff members were overawed. It became a moment that I hope has an effect on my son's, and perhaps the shop staff's, Integritude.

To work this Attitude Shifter, I challenge you to take every opportunity to enhance your integrity. It WILL have impact on those around you.

In the hardware store where the check-out staff only spot five of the six sheets of plasterboard, tell them. Where litter lies near the bin, pick it up and dispose it. When you find coins, put them in the next charity pot. If you say you'll do something or be at the meeting, be there (or don't say it!). Replace the loo roll if you use the last sheet. Hold your tongue when a gossip moment arrives.

The seemingly irrelevant moments for Integrity Enhancement can accumulate fast!

HIGH INTEGRITY LIES
AT THE HEART OF POWERFUL
AND EFFECTIVE ATTITUDES.

22.
POKER FACE

In poker, when your opponents are scanning and studying you deeply, they would say they are attempting to read your 'tell'. In your everyday life, when the focus on you may be almost as intense, your 'tells' are detectable. If they aren't consistent with your projected attitude, they may be blurring your message or even confusing your audience.

Your attitude communicates, you cannot conceal what goes on inside.

Most of your messaging will be in the middle, both you and they won't consciously detect your attitude signs, but your message will not have the impact you intend, as your underlying attitude 'tells' grin through. If you are harbouring anger, resentment, joy, relief, freedom, anxiety, or perhaps even a curious concoction of a few of these, you communicate them to the world.

It takes a disproportionate amount of energy to communicate a message that is disconnected from what's actually going on inside.

You are a wonderful human, changing your thoughts and the corresponding emotional range is not as simple as a single flicked-switch. Here are three attitude shifts to sharpen your impact and get you to communicate what you truly intend.

● ● ●

● ● ●

a) **Chill** – relax; specifically your face, neck and back muscles. Breathe slowly and deliberately a few times, fill the lungs fully, hold briefly and fully exhale. This begins to unravel the body's response to your angst and the accumulated effect of carrying that emotion for a while.

b) **Return** – be here now, come back from wherever your thoughts are dragging you. Notice five things around you, sounds, sights, smells, and appreciate them for what they are. This is a step toward the more mindful version of you.

c) **Smile** – hold that smile for at least 10 seconds, even if you are on your own. This jolts the brain, which at first may try to defy the suggested change of mood.

And, if you are carrying an inner set of emotions that are still loud after this shift:

Be Honest, Be Humble, Be Distinct.

Share with your audience your inner emotion set, what is going on behind your desired attitude and accept that it may impair your message, separate the two and give yourself permission to get back on message.

IT TAKES A DISPROPORTIONATE
AMOUNT OF ENERGY TO
COMMUNICATE A MESSAGE THAT
IS DISCONNECTED FROM WHAT'S
ACTUALLY GOING ON INSIDE.

23.
FAKE TRUTH

Fears and doubts nibble away at your positive attitude, testing your attitudinal resilience.

But are your current fears really true? Are they actually as bad, intense, busy, overwhelming, difficult and complicated as you are telling yourself (repeatedly and often unconsciously)?

It just might not be true, but it feels enough like it could be for you to persist with the thought and the ensuing attitude that it triggers.

I sometimes notice I have become entangled in one of my own fake truths when my mood has slipped down the range. The attitude I shift to is grumpy, grouchy or grizzly and my energy reserves quickly drain. At this point, it is too tough to simply think my way through and out of the fog!

a) Call a time-out, grab a pen and paper, step aside, go somewhere away from 'the action'. What are you actually carrying as your current truth? Write it down, describing as best you can your current predicament and experience.

b) Pause and contemplate what else might be true? Could there be counter evidence? How much of your experience is of your own interpretation? Write down the counter evidence, the best you can, and pause again.

c) What 'truth' would you prefer, honestly? How would you prefer to work today? What version of you would you want to show up today?

• • •

• • •

If you act chaotically you will absolutely prove to yourself that chaos is all around you and your attitude will spiral accordingly. If you wear a frown most days and grit your teeth, most events you encounter will be consistent with this mask-set.

Change it, it might be fake truth!

FEARS AND DOUBTS NIBBLE
AWAY AT YOUR POSITIVE
ATTITUDE, TESTING YOUR
ATTITUDINAL RESILIENCE.

24.
CELEBRATIONS

Change, of any nature, always feels better if it's worth it, even more so if it is to be sustainable. Our effort and input requires some kind of return on investment for our body and mind to make energy continually available.

In situations where the next demanding task arrives before the last is completed, and no time is allowed to come up for air or to even notice the successful application of the previous efforts, resilience levels erode. Attitudes drop and motivational remedies (affirmation words, rewards, money) become impotent.

On your attitude journey, taking action with the shifters in this book will give you new results and they may, at times, be positively significant! Well done. Before turning the page and working on the next chapter, pause for a moment and celebrate the change.

I take inspiration from Ken Blanchard and Spencer Johnson's classic management book *The One Minute Manager* (perhaps one of the most successful management books ever published!), which simply and concisely presents the concepts of one-minute goals; one-minute praisings and one-minute reprimands.

For this Attitude Shifter, I encourage you to emulate their book and add 'one-minute celebrations'. As with goals, praisings and reprimands, the celebration should be proportional and in relation to the achievement.

● ● ●

● ● ●

a) Create and draw up a scaled list of potential celebrations – a treat, a moment of relaxation, some R&R, a brief indulgence, that clothing item you've had your eye on, a weekend away.
b) Go about your journey, noticing what is worthy of a celebration.
c) Take the celebration, enjoy the moment, perhaps write about it, and move on.

It's because you're worth it!

ON YOUR ATTITUDE JOURNEY,
TAKING ACTION WITH THE SHIFTERS
IN THIS BOOK WILL GIVE YOU NEW
RESULTS AND THEY MAY, AT TIMES,
BE POSITIVELY SIGNIFICANT!

25.
RESOURCE
LIBRARY

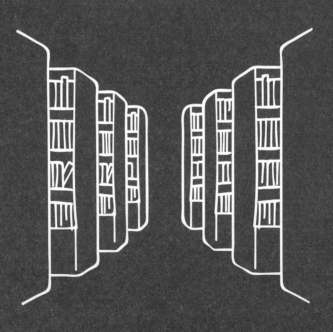

Imagine the luxury of having a cupboard stuffed full of everything you need, all sorted and organized for quick access.

What might be in that bountiful store?

PEOPLE

DATA

CONTACT INFORMATION

TIME

IDEAS

FEEL-GOOD VITAMINS

HEALTH

RELAXATION

REWARDS

ENCOURAGEMENT

EXTRA TIME

ROUTES

ORGANIZERS

ALTERNATIVES

NICE PLACES TO VISIT

BEAUTIFUL SCENERY

INTERNET SPEED

FRIENDS

INSIGHTFUL CRITIQUES

HAZARD WARNINGS

RELIEF PACKAGES

HELP FOR THOSE

IMPORTANT TO YOU

RESCUERS

LOAD-CARRIERS

FINANCE

DETAIL CHECKERS

PREPARED MEALS

TRAINERS

MOTIVATORS

INSPIRERS

COACHES

INTELLIGENCE

EXPERIENCE

TESTERS AND TRAILERS

VOLUNTEERS

SIMPLIFIERS

OFFICE EQUIPMENT

COMFORT

ATTITUDES

• • •

● ● ●

Scan through this list again and indulge, add to your own perfect resource library. Consider what and who would be usefully there, for any situation you have faced or might face, good, bad, challenging, whatever.

Just think what could you be capable of if you had easy access to such abundant resources? Who could you be? What could be possible? What excuses would vaporize and how powerful and confident you would feel?

a) Read your Resource Library list again (my list, plus whatever you have added), noting whether you have that item in stock now or not. If yes – describe how well it currently works and where it is.
b) Highlight the missing resources and spend time over the next month finding them or finding routes to them.
c) Remind yourself often that the library is yours with full free access – and use it!

Spending time compiling or gazing into your resource library will gently boost your attitude; each time you use something from your wonderful storeroom the boost will be received again.

IMAGINE THE LUXURY OF HAVING
A CUPBOARD STUFFED FULL OF
EVERYTHING YOU NEED, ALL SORTED
AND ORGANIZED FOR QUICK ACCESS.

26.
HISTORY
REWRITTEN

Your personal history tends to provide an expectation for your future and a boundary to the range into which your future might expand.

In some cases, depending on what you have encountered, survived and grown through, this can be useful and encouraging, even motivational. In other cases your history may perhaps be more restrictive than helpful. I have observed that histories can constrain creative ambition and haul us back from what we may deem to be reckless or truly 'not meant for us'.

Each time you think about or retell your history it is likely to, at best, be a balance between the good and the bad, the triumphant and the woeful, and sometimes, depending on your prevailing attitude, you may dwell on the glum.

a) How do you retell your personal history? What stories have come to define you? What aspects of your history play out today, every day?
b) Separate out the chapters that feel good and motivational from those that don't – respectfully store the latter and decide now not to refer to them or allow them be right at the surface of your story.
c) Re-write the bad ones in inspiring ways, in terms of how they were actually positive, how they have helped you become who you are today, and how they helped and served you.

Rewrite your personal history and know that your early passes at thinking or telling this upgraded story will feel a little difficult, until they don't!

27.
ATTITUDE
BUFFER

> **Buffer**
>
> *noun* – A person or thing that reduces a shock or that forms a barrier between incompatible or antagonistic people or things. "family and friends can provide a buffer against stress"
> *synonyms*: cushion, bulwark
>
> *verb* – To lessen or moderate the impact of (something). "the massage helped to buffer the strain"

Sometimes you don't get to choose the environment in which you work or the people in that environment. That environment may contain irritants, antagonizers and folk that have their own attitudes, behaviours, opinions and ways of working, and the impact that has on you and your opinions may be incompatible. Often you will notice the change in your behaviour, you may lose focus, feel doubt, fear, uncertainty, anxiety and lose determination. Your wonderful skills and abilities seem to retreat.

So, a buffer can be useful, every now and then, to protect you against the waves of incompatibility and antagonism! Here are the **10 settings** of the Attitude Buffer:

1. Notice them. Just the act of reading this Attitude Shifter will allow your mind to auto-buffer.
2. Manage your time. Minimize your exposure to those places and people that need buffering. Shorten planned meetings to 45 minutes instead of 60, avoid back-to-back battles.

● ● ●

• • •

3. Take a break. There are many ways to finesse this. Go for a walk, breathe, meditate, read or write for 10 minutes.
4. Find a buffer buddy. Some people simply make you feel good, put the world to rights and have a happy infectious attitude. Be with them and thank them!
5. Remember who you are. Write down your goal, your intention and the reason why you do what you do. And carry that note with you for referral under pressure.
6. Relax (consciously). Anxiety triggers tightening of muscles. Practice switching your anxiety-response muscles off (shoulders, jaw, neck etc.)
7. Take a Translator! There may be someone in your team who naturally connects more effectively with someone than you. Take them with you, not all messages need to come from you.
8. Toughen resilience. The better shape you are in physically, mentally, spiritually, the more resilient you are to the opposites. Look after yourself.
9. Face It. Those that cause something in you often have something to teach you. Work with a buddy or a coach to explore what it may be.
10. Change them. This is the abrupt one! If you have been working with antagonizers for a while and nothing is changing, it may be time to accept the situation and change them (terminate clients, stakeholders etc.!)

Your attitude will already have shifted and your ability to choose what it will now become has returned.

A BUFFER CAN BE USEFUL, EVERY NOW AND THEN, TO PROTECT YOU AGAINST THE WAVES OF INCOMPATIBILITY AND ANTAGONISM!

28.
THE SEVEN

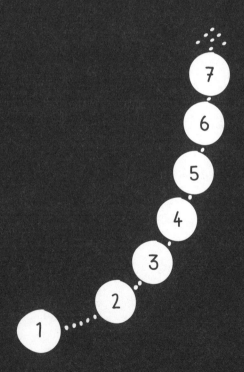

In all my client work, coaching, facilitating and speaking, I have become increasingly aware of the attitude individuals carry that reflects the particular phase of their career or the challenges that at that time engulf them.

Many factors influence your state and attitude; pressures and demands, volume of work, the mood and conditions of your environment, recent performance and results (good or bad). I have identified seven distinct attitude sets that are present in anyone's work journey.

To identify your attitude, first spend a few moments defining your present state. The accumulation of external issues and pressures combine to alter your mind set, mood, attitude, expectations, confidence and decision-making. This perpetuates the attitude-state and can create a feeling of 'being stuck', later becoming entrenched as the new self-belief (or self-doubt).

Being unaware of the state and taking no action means you are prone to slip down the Seven scale! The notional titles I have chosen for the Seven are to capture the feelings that are likely to be experienced there. Make a mental note of which state reflects your current situation and attitude:

● ● ●

• • •

- **'On Top'** – literally on top of your game, ample awareness of what is going on, where you are headed, synthesizing many peripheral pieces of information into brilliant and clear leadership.
- **'In Control'** – all bases covered, strong momentum, delivering to expectations.
- **'Holding it Together'** – having to and being capable of reacting to sudden changes, unexpected new demands, lots of energy (and time) required.
- **'Holding On'** – it doesn't quite feel like enough time in the day or sufficient resources to hold everything, intense everyday pressure to remember everything. It seems most activity is manual, nothing is automated; draining.
- **'Clinging On'** – it feels like too much, increased errors and corrective/fix actions, repeat work. Relationships suffer, conversations are more clipped.
- **'Falling Apart'** – missing things, increasing self-doubt, fatigue, irrational behaviour moments, relationship and communication mistakes and breakdowns.
- **'Lost It'** – it's now remedial, huge doubt leads to a feeling of defeat, giving up, retrenching, scorn, bad moods, affecting others.

Where are you on this list? Simply making time to identify your status on your own, with a buddy or as a team, can be enough to get you started on raising your attitude set.

Decide to shift your attitude to the next state up, in spite of prevailing conditions, get support, build resilience, adapt and press on.

29.
THE 'YOU'
BOARD OF
DIRECTORS

The busier you get, the more consumed you may become by the complexities of your life, your intentions may become obscured and your attitude will be at risk!

What you spend your time on, where your focus goes, can often be overwhelmingly driven by the situation. As you become immersed in the urgent demands of projects, people, customers, you may become reactive and lose sight of your positive, deliberate choices.

The 'You' Board Attitude Shifter inserts a pause in activity, alters the view on your current situation and investigates your attitudes.

Broadly speaking, corporations across the world have a board of directors to provide accountability on:
- **Performance** – consistency and direction.
- **Strategy** – policies and objectives.
- **Resources** – acquisition and alignment.

And I want that for you, on behalf of You Inc, You pty or You plc!

Assemble your board and hold a meeting. The executive seats at the boardroom table of Company You each have their own distinct role and goal. It might only be at your board meeting that the quieter directors regain their voice and get heard!

• • •

●●●

Spend five minutes with each of your director roles, consider their objective and how they would view you, what might they want you to focus on or put effort into now?

CHIEF EXECUTIVE YOU
How are you doing?
What results can you report?
What lies ahead?
What are the challenges you currently face?

CHIEF FINANCIAL YOU
What is the state of your personal finance?
Where are the risks?
Where is investment needed?
Controls needed?

CHIEF OPERATING YOU
How well are you getting 'the job' done?
Are you delivering, on time, adding value?

HR YOU
How is your talent being accessed, nurtured, expanded?
How is your health and wellness and ability to perform?

CHIEF MARKETING YOU
What is your brand now?
How well is it known and being cleanly and consistently communicated?

For full effect, invite a trusted facilitator to the board meeting dialogue. This process is essential in lifting what is truly important for you up and out of the everyday operationally urgent busyness.

I have found the virtual conversation with these five directors enough for me to review and realign my journey often. Your circumstances may further benefit from other roles (IT, Community, PR), so engage them as you need to build a strong 'You' Board of directors.

30.
SIMPLY
AWESOME

Creating, tuning into and expanding your sense of awe is one of the most liberating and relief-providing remedies I can prescribe.

When times are tough, your attitude dips and you feel the grip of concentration or just the grip of concern, your ability to notice the awesome in anything wanes. Your ego kicks in and steers your thinking, you may feel more fearful and drift from mini-disaster to aggravating relationship to disappointing event.

A former coaching teacher and mentor of mine, Jay Perry would often say: *"There is an awesome in every awful!"* This challenge is precisely what I throw at you in this Attitude Shifter.

Finding the awesome around you loosens the hold of the ego, staves off disasters and can liberate you from fear. It works every time. Furthermore, being in a state of awe diminishes the chances of experiencing boredom or disappointment.

So, here's my challenge ...

Right now, find five natural occurrences in your daily life. Occurrences that perhaps you have taken for granted up until now.

● ● ●

● ● ●

For a few moments, consider the awesomeness of the sky, the plants and wildlife around you, the wind, rain, sun, a cobweb, grass between paving stones, the people walking by. Expand your ability to observe awesome as you repeat this exercise, to include anything you notice, technology, buildings, machinery, constructions, the thought that went behind them, etc. No judgments, just capture the awesome.

Return to this exercise whenever the grip of ego returns and at least once a day. In doing so, you will not become weary, in fact you are likely to shift your attitude significantly upwards each time and soon everyday could be simply awesome!

"THERE IS AN AWESOME
IN EVERY AWFUL!"
JAY PERRY

31.
CALL OFF
THE SEARCH

Every day you will receive a constant delivery of new things – people, chances, challenges, information and choices. All of them potentially exciting, uplifting opportunities, but possibly boring, draining and heavy loads. It may feel as if you are stuck on life's hamster wheel, repeating patterns, but new is there, better is possible, all the time.

Largely dependent on your attitude, sometimes you notice and grasp these passing memes, sometimes you don't.

And yet we persist with searching, the desperate craving for new and better things. Could this be impairing you? Even when new or better arrives, if it doesn't exactly match the unconscious, artificial nirvana you have created in your mind, you'll let it go by.

All the time you are on the seeking journey, you add stress, doubt, anger and a range of emotions relating to how much you hate your current situation and how much you desperately seek the new.

Oprah Winfrey brilliantly spoke to this point: *"Be thankful for what you have; you'll end up having more. If you concentrate on what you don't have, you will never, ever have enough."*

● ● ●

• • •

To get off the craving path, upgrade your attitude and begin to attract and notice incredible new and better options effortlessly and automatically:

a) Connect to what you have right now. I mean everything. Your experiences, your physical capabilities, your intellectual capacity, your possessions, your connections, the relationships you currently have (irrespective of what you have been telling yourself about them). List them, right now, on paper.

b) Cease pining for new, step back into what you have, hug it, cherish it, love it, be it and do it a bit more today. Initially it may feel like you're closing out to new or better, but this is absolutely not the case.

c) Be open to noticing what starts to show up from this point.

From here onwards, things will become easier and simpler and the door to new and better is open.

I repeat again: new and better is arriving all the time, on its own, nothing to do with you. Stop seeking, call off the search.

IT MAY FEEL AS IF YOU ARE
STUCK ON LIFE'S HAMSTER WHEEL,
REPEATING PATTERNS,
BUT NEW IS THERE, BETTER IS
POSSIBLE, ALL THE TIME.

32.
MAGNETS

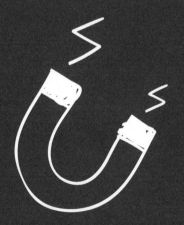

We humans are magnetic, we are electrical energy emitting and receiving all the time. We are able to attract to us a range of things: people; incidences; opportunities; new thoughts that are aligned to our existing thoughts; behaviour and activity up to and including that moment.

And, just like a magnet, with its two opposite poles, when turned the other way around we repel opposites.

The simplest way to work with this magnet attitude shifter is to check the magnet and pole as it is functioning for you right now:

a) Consider what you are attracting and, conversely, what you seem to be repelling.
b) Contrast these results with the sorts of things, events, people that you would rather be attracting (or repelling!).
c) Design the corresponding version of you (in attitude and behaviour) that is more aligned with the desired results.

Redefine and redirect your magnetic force.

33.
KNOW WHERE
YOU'RE GOING

When I visit bustling city centres, I am always amused by the attitudes and moods I notice around me. Particularly at transport hubs, stations and airports. I find reading people easier in these places.

The way people hold themselves, the pace at which they walk, the lines or curves they travel, hand movements, where they gaze, the urgency with which they seem to be conversing; all clues to what is probably going on for them.

After a while, I'm sure I could guess, to a fair degree of accuracy, who knows where they are going; who is looking forward to getting there; who is behind schedule; what attitude they are holding.

This Attitude Shifter is a challenge for you, for when the moment arrives: carry yourself like you know where you are going!

The attitude that corresponds to this state is distinct and obvious, exudes confidence and assurance and, in leadership terms, is most likely to attract followers.

If you were to carry yourself like you knew where you were going consider your:
- **Pace** – even, not slow and not fast.
- **Posture** – balanced and tall, no stoop and not bolt upright.
- **Hands** – relaxed and free.
- **Face** – calm, easy smile.
- **Gaze** – mainly forward but comfortably taking in surroundings.

Use a mirror to practise and walk on!

34.
A THOUSAND
THANK YOUS

This attitude shifter works well in conjunction with **Attitude Shifter #5 – Gratitude** (p18).

The more widely I read and research, the more I find new evidence confirming the positive effect of gratitude.

Among other revelations, a study at UC Davis Health by Robert Emmons (editor of *The Journal of Positive Psychology* and author of *Gratitude Works*) reported a 28% reduction in perceived stress and 23% lower levels of the stress hormone cortisol.

The intention to up our gratitude performance rises and falls; as our attitude meets tough times, gratitude becomes contingent on how our attitude is set up!

To work your attitude muscle, try this: starting on Monday next week, begin the Thousand Thank You Challenge and deliver 1,000 thank yous in a calendar month. That's roughly 33 per day. Keep a log to track your progress.

This challenge is likely to be a scale jump from even your most thankful monthly norms. So you will need to extend and develop new thank you strategies.

● ● ●

● ● ●

Opportunities for thank yous exist everywhere once you start looking; retail and hospitality time; people that hold a door, make way for you in traffic; noticing someone in the act of a valiant or worthy task; etc.

Ensure you keep your thank yous proportional to each act worth thanking, I advise the following delivery standards:

a) **Heard** – be clear and articulate.
b) **Sincere** – with meaning and relevance.
c) **With a smile** – be you.

Your attitude will shift as you near your 1,000 target ... be grateful!

THE MORE WIDELY I READ
AND RESEARCH, THE MORE I FIND
NEW EVIDENCE CONFIRMING THE
POSITIVE EFFECT OF GRATITUDE.

35.
VOCABITUDE

Attitudes influence an incredible amount of our body, mind and spirit. An attitude that we have been holding for a sustained period of time can dictate our stature, our thinking and actions.

When I am observing teams and executive boards, a reliable window onto their attitudes is the words I hear them using to describe issues and situations.

Vocabitude is the lexicon of words we use with each attitude.

If you are despondent and gloomy, your brain will push certain vocabulary to the front and you will find yourself using words such as loss; defeat; pointless; whatever; don't know; don't care; why; why not and no!

If you are full of energy, confidence and belief, your words are more likely to include can; will; let's; how; what; possible; chance; and yes!

a) Over the week ahead, tune in to the words of others when you know the mood and attitude they are in, then tune into your own.
b) Develop your Vocabitude – the words you use when you are at the top of your attitude range.
c) Have them to hand when you are feeling off beat and insert them in your written and spoken conversations (especially if, at first, they feel incongruous to your bad mood).

Give your attitude a great script.

36.
SCANNERS

What are you looking at, what do you notice, what appears on your radar or scanner screen?

The attitude you are carrying right now affects many aspects of the version of you that is showing up, specifically:

- How your thoughts flow.
- The nature of the new thoughts that arrive.
- The words that come to mind and are articulated.
- What you are drawn to.
- What you are repelled by and from.
- What you notice.

This shifter focuses on the latter. Your scanner or radar.

To protect you from sensory overload, you have in-built filters that select and highlight what you actually see, aligned with what your brain has picked up as being important or necessary for you today – i.e. your attitude!

a) What are you noticing that piques your interest, captures your emotions and causes a reaction in you?
b) Compare and contrast this with what you would like to be noticing that would support and enhance your upgraded attitude (e.g. if you were blissfully happy what would you be noticing, dwelling on, cherishing?).
c) Actively and deliberately seek out those, until now, previously unnoticed things.

Your attitude will have no choice but to shift and realign with what you are now scanning and soon the scanner will be finding the good stuff on its own.

37.
REACTION
FREE

How we react to everyday stimuli is a clue to the attitude we currently have set in place.

What thoughts are ignited when you notice:
- Errors.
- People different from you.
- Mistakes made by others.
- Process and system breakdown.
- Flaws and weaknesses.
- Queues and delays.
- Slips and falls.
- Noises.

Your huffing reaction of annoyance, anger, complaint or fury will be unhelpful and does not remedy the situation, it damages only you.

I challenge you to a 24-hour period of being Reaction Free!

Whenever you meet with a provoker:

a) Breathe in deeply and out slowly.
b) Count to three.
c) Release the reaction as it arrives.

This will unlock your poorly set-up stimuli-response pattern and return you to a calmer state. From there, you are attitude-neutral and ready to begin again.

38.
CYCLING
TRUTHS

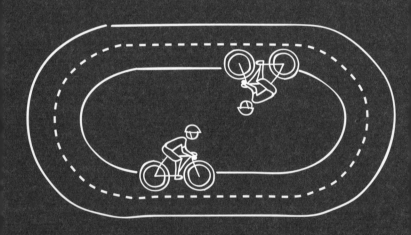

I have admired author, speaker and entrepreneur Mike Dooley for many years, and often refer to one of his signature statements, *"Thoughts become things."* It captures how our thoughts, however randomly originated, when held and thought about further, soon develop into more tangible concepts and eventually become a 'thing'.

When your attitude is set, it tends to operate as a range-finder frame for thoughts. When a thought comes to mind that is outside of your attitude frame, you will be briefly perplexed and most often let it go. When a thought arrives that fits inside the frame, you will grasp it more firmly and hold it (and turn it into a 'thing') confirming and locking in your attitude (and its boundaried framework) further.

Thus we set up a cycle of (presumed) truths, 'this' (the new thought) leads to a justified 'then' (it must be true!).

This cycle of truths holds you in the framework and your attitude becomes set.

This is brilliant when your attitude is desirable and helping you be positive, happy and successful. Where it is not, change is required, the truth cycle needs interruption and positive defiance.

If things aren't working out for you exactly as you would hope, the next (presumed) truth that you will cycle won't alter that, rather it will confirm that things aren't working out. Which means that you will react with reluctant melancholic acceptance that

• • •

● ● ●

these are your truths. Your attitude becomes unhelpful and your truth cycle takes you downhill fast.

Attitude shift and insert a new truth, which doesn't need to be contrary to what seems to be true, instead it is an 'alternate truth', a new angle on the same situation. For example: Things work out or they teach me. I learn no matter what' or 'that's interesting, what can I learn or notice here' or 'everything is okay'.

Challenging at first, this may take several repetitions to interrupt the cycle. Write down your truth cycle interrupter as a reminder. Eventually the direction will change and your attitude will rise again.

"THOUGHTS BECOME THINGS."

MIKE DOOLEY

39.
SCENE
SELECTOR

In the TV and film industry, studios across the world, producers, editors, directors are cutting and splicing already shot scenes to create the next blockbuster.

Some scenes will have been filmed several times, in different ways, from different angles, with different emphasis. Occasionally the sequence will be changed from the original scripted order as they enhance the impact it will have on the storyline. And some scenes are dropped altogether and destined only for the studio cutting floor.

Sometimes the media industry has, as a result of various contractual, legal or scandal-related issues, had to remove an actor from the cast, meaning an entire reshoot of scenes with the replacement crew.

In your own story, the way you describe it and replay it, reflect on it and use it to influence your decisions, expectations and attitudes, could be very similar.

I'm not suggesting a complete fictional rewrite, I'm inviting you to spend some time thinking about your existing footage and upgrade your Scene Selector exactly as a leading executive producer would.

● ● ●

• • •

What memories would you like to access that would boost your attitude, not diminish it. Prepare the scene – most of it has already been shot!

I notice that the movie production teams have four main options:

1. Multiple takes with alternative angles/views/emphasis.
2. Change the sequence.
3. Switch actors.
4. Cut unneeded scenes that don't help the storyline.

The same options exist for you, so to work through this attitude shifter:

a) What is your current story, scene by scene?
b) Identify the scenes that take your attitude down and just don't feel good.
c) Use the producer's Scene Selector toolkit and re-edit.

It's your story, select the blockbuster version!

SPEND SOME TIME THINKING
ABOUT YOUR EXISTING FOOTAGE
AND UPGRADE YOUR SCENE
SELECTOR EXACTLY AS A LEADING
EXECUTIVE PRODUCER WOULD.

40.
HERE AND
THERE

Every now and then, I experience a 'eureka' or an 'aha' moment, having discovered a new insight into attitude, impact, simplicity, the meaning of life and everything. Once the euphoric glow has begun to dim, it is replaced with excitement about how I can share it and get the new discovery into abundant use.

These moments tend to pass within a few hours (or days if the insight is higher up on my notional scale of life-changing profoundness) and I return to a similar but thought-expanded place from whence I came. The success I have had with these insights has been when I have used 'Here and There' on my accompanying attitude.

Inherent in any effective change, goal setting, purpose seeking and attitude shifting is the ability to view yourself, your team, or your company from 'over there' (as if it were true already). The more excitement, joy, desire, passion that can be ignited in connection with that future, the deeper it will penetrate your present attitudes, thoughts, feelings and actions.

A by-product of future gazing is that it can create disappointment with now, the current state. Noticing what's missing can take away the excitement and joy that existed when you were painting the future. In extreme cases, this can lead to pointlessness, learned hopelessness and reluctant glum acceptance of your current situation.

● ● ●

• • •

Instead, hold the good feelings experienced while future gazing for a little longer (don't hastily jump back to the present moment as soon as a new future-sourced idea has formed). Pause and bring them back with you into the now. I suggest you ask and answer three questions:

a) What exists right now that is similar to and could be the seeds for that future?
b) What is great about now?
c) What is true already?

A phrase I have caught myself espousing often is: *"You can only get more of what you've got already."* If you are full of disappointment, lack, scarcity right now, that influences your attitude and is likely what you will attract. Almost defying old logic, the art of celebrating 'now' has immense accelerating power, builds belief and supports attitudes of happiness and success, already!

GOAL SETTING, PURPOSE SEEKING AND
ATTITUDE SHIFTING IS THE ABILITY TO
VIEW YOURSELF, YOUR TEAM, OR YOUR
COMPANY FROM 'OVER THERE'.

41.
START A FIRE

A roaring fire gives warmth, light and a source of power to heat and cook food. The reds, oranges and yellows of the flames are irresistibly alluring and draw people near.

When your attitude is at its roaring best, you are that fire. Your warmth and light are just as powerful and alluring.

Perhaps, then, the components of your mood and attitude are like the logs, branches and sticks of a would-be fire. Unlit, they are dormant, latent energy givers. Wood (or attitudes) that are damp or covered in accumulated moss and weeds (doubt, nay-sayers), or are too young and green (not fully thought-through or believed) are extremely difficult to light. Wood in that condition is best left to dry and 'cure' or only added to an already established fire.

A good fire needs to be started. Dry kindling, easily lit, well placed, and requires only a spark of ignition, not a glug of hazardous, toxic but ultimately effective petroleum (relying on external forces and situations for your attitude to ignite).

Note: I have noticed over the years that fires started with fuel tend to reek of that fuel for a long while, even after the fire is established.

Start your fire:
- **Kindling** = your passions, beliefs, certainties.
- **Spark** = your active and deliberate attitude choice.
- **Fan the flame** = music, people, attitude shifters.
- **Add dry logs** = brave steps, places, tell and involve others (bigger logs can be added once your fire has been established).

42.
SH*T
HAPPENS

Even with all this positive strengthening work you are committing to regarding your attitude; even with the improving range of incidences and events that you are now attracting with your enhanced attitude; even then... sh*t still happens.

Forgive my use of this obscenity, its everyday vernacular use captures this shifter.

I have had a tiny sign displaying the exact statement in my fish tank for many years and, each time I catch sight of it, I smile, as I am reminded again of the truism!

For fish, as with me, it's not what happens, it's how I respond to what happens that maintains or dents my attitude.

In the early phases of your attitude improvement journey, if 'it' happens, it can hit hard, deflect you from you attitudinal course and into 'it' you'll fall.

It happens, that's the truth, and, on most occasions, it has absolutely nothing to do with you.

Your attitude resilience may need reminding that 'Sh*t Happens'.

a) **Notice it**.
b) **Disengage** (it has nothing to do with you).
c) **Work through it**, without letting it affect your attitude.

Bad things happen – select neutral before it takes hold and shifts your attitude.

43.
MOMENTS

When it comes down to it, that's all life is – moments. A series of moments that you string together to form your experience, your story and your memories. The quality of the moments you choose, actively or passively, correlates with the attitudes you have carried and determines the theme of your story.

As life's intensity shifts, as your relationships and your work become more complex, you may often get lost in the stressful demands and shift to a reactive mode delivering to the loudest shout. Your attitude and activity is at the behest of the urgent slide deck, the imminent pitch, the early start, the demanding call, the impending decision, giving a feeling of tension and concern often described as the metaphorical 'burning bridge'.

What gets lost in that wired state is the beauty and spectacle of your moments ... the important stuff hidden behind the screaming urgencies. Here the moments are less than joyful and can stretch over hours and days, immensely draining and unfulfilling!

With this everyday expectation and pressure to perform, compete, impress and survive, you lose your innate moment-noticing skills through lack of presence, lack of attention to this actual moment, right now. Your thinking and attitude become lodged 'over there,' somewhere where moments don't happen.

The skill of noticing works with the ability to be 'in the now' and being in the now enhances your abilities to notice moments. And what you notice supports and strengthens your attitude and boosts your attitude resilience.

● ● ●

• • •

Moments to notice are your choice, get active. Notice the nice ones. They are happening anyway. And they aren't necessarily spectacular fanfare moments, grand-vista moments, worthy of an artist's brush or an orchestra's crescendo. They can be as simple as that brief rush of feeling good that triggers the body's production of its feel-good chemical, serotonin.

Once you've retrained your moment-catching skills, you may be astounded how many there are.

An inspirational challenge from Eckhart Tolle: *"What happens if you accept this moment."* Accepting this moment for what it is instantly releases resistance and friction and heightens our awareness of right now. (See **Further Reading**, p170).

MOMENTS...
THAT'S WHY WE ARE HERE.

44.
LOOM

Perhaps the most dampening of all feelings on my own attitude-resilience journey has been 'loom'.

Loom is what I describe as the dark, heavy sensation that is linked to a 'looming' significant deadline or commitment or requirement to which I feel little or no joy. In the past it has been a tax bill, a critically important deadline, an imminent difficult conversation or decision. If there's more than one loom item present, the effect is massively multiplied.

Loom will impair your ability to concentrate for extended periods of time. Loom makes a happy smile incongruous and often out of reach. Tempers fray, creativity is stifled, capacity and willingness for new things is almost nil. Attitudes slide to a broad malaise of unhappiness.

Loom does not naturally go away. After the causal deadline has passed, the dulled mood can hang on longer. Loom requires proper processing, i.e. the work/deadline needs to be completed and achieved OR our attitude to it needs to change, now.

As you start work on shifting your loom-infected attitude, you will not, at first, believe the alternatives as being plausible or realistic. You will find motivation to persist difficult, but not impossible to access. Breathe deep, take time.

● ● ●

· · ·

a) **Everything is okay**. You will get through this, you always have, and will again.
b) Go to your Resource Library (**Attitude Shifter #25**, p86).
c) Look at your week ahead, be realistic about the time you will spend focusing on your loom, schedule it and relax, even just a little, knowing that you are on the case.

Grant yourself permission to live a loom-free life!

LOOM DOES NOT NATURALLY
GO AWAY. [...] LOOM REQUIRES
PROPER PROCESSING.

45.
TOUGHEST
CHALLENGE
FIRST

Once your attitude is positively and deliberately set for the day ahead, depending on its strength and your resilience, you can use it to plough through challenging situations, conversations and whatever life throws at you.

If you've worked with the Attitude Shifters in this book to build both your attitude and your resilience, it is likely that you will now be at your attitude-strongest in the early part of the day. That's the time when you could face any challenge, more effectively than times when your energy levels have lessened.

It is a no-brainer, but many I have worked with admit to putting off the tough stuff until 'the perfect time' or have brilliant excuses for delay as they wait for 'a little bit more information'.

The euphoric hit you get from completing the tough stuff actually boosts your attitude, so experiment with this shift and focus on the Toughest Challenge First.

a) Identify the task/project/conversation or challenge that weighs you down, that you have spent time procrastinating about (proactive sales call, planning the month ahead etc.).
b) Make it the first thing you do every day (but be sensitive to yourself, just plan to get on with it for 10 minutes – if you go on, it's a bonus).
c) Reward yourself immediately after (drinks break, quiet time, etc.).

Your attitude will already have shifted and your ability to choose what it can now become has been boosted.

46.
PEAK TIME

We tend to pay significantly more for tickets at peak times compared with off-peak times. Market forces are at play – demand is higher and the price is less sensitive.

This metaphor can apply to you – you have a peak and an off-peak version of you (attitude, energy, behaviour). Get to know this and your value and perhaps even your pricing can follow the metaphor too!

Have you ever monitored when you feel at your physical peak, and when you don't? Have you considered the times in the day or week when you are better at thinking or better at writing or better at articulating to colleagues?

Until you do, you may be holding expectations and demands that are too high, setting yourself up for disappointment and an attitude drop.

There are likely to be regular recurring times during a day when, biologically, you are at your best and other times when you are at lower ebbs (physically, emotionally, and mentally).

● ● ●

• • •

a) Observe yourself over the next few days. Notice patterns that may be linked to food and water intake or the environments you are in or the people you are with.
b) Identify and trial the peak-times of the day that you push yourself to the limits, get involved in deeper and demanding work. These are the times when your attitude can shine and be in full effect.
c) Identify and trial your off-peak times to schedule more appropriate activities, meetings with colleagues, reading, email clearance, etc. These are the times when you are more gentle with yourself and your attitude.

Match your day and week with your peak-times.

THERE ARE LIKELY TO BE REGULAR RECURRING TIMES DURING A DAY WHEN BIOLOGICALLY YOU ARE AT YOUR BEST AND OTHER TIMES WHEN YOU ARE AT LOWER EBBS.

47.
DAILY
INTENTIONS

Until you decide, and become deliberate and determined, you remain susceptible to the flotsam and jetsam of the day ahead.

One of my heroes, the late Dr Wayne W. Dyer, elaborately and inspirationally wrote about this in his book *The Power of Intention*. We all have intentions at play all the time about our life, our relationships, our career and even our day ahead. But, in most cases, when unarticulated, our intentions are unclear, unworded and a mish-mash of what we want, what we hope, what we don't want, what we'll accept and so on.

Intentions don't necessarily mean 'make five calls' or 'make the sale'. An intention is more about the impact you want to have, the state you plan to be in, the attitude you would want to hold.

a) Consider what lies ahead today, what is it that you want to happen, who do you want to be/need to be?
b) Write it down and keep it visible or in easy reach, perhaps on the back of a business card or clip it to your PC screen.
c) Read and remind yourself of your intention when you feel off-course.

Set your intention and let go of it! Gripping tightly to an intention makes it a 'have to', which closes down other new options, or better and different things. Hold your intentions lightly.

The act of thinking about your intentions often is enough to shift your attitude and set in motion coincidences, meetings, moments and events that might not otherwise have happened or been noticed. Writing them down and reviewing them often raises the likelihood of these upgraded experiences.

48.
GO TO
THE EDGE

When someone takes on a new role or moves to a new location (rarely more than one variable changes at a time!) the newness soon wears off and that too becomes part of their known comfortable and largely predictable circle.

Each time you go to and stay at your edge (rather than feeling the discomfort and immediately retreating to the safe and known) you ignite part of your creative subconscious and become more awake, alert and all senses engage. Collecting information, reviewing previous data, assessing who you are now, how are you doing, what is working, what needs change. This is healthy!

Going To The Edge tests, exercises and stretches your attitude muscles.

a) Where are the edges of your comfort zone today, the places where you feel your skill and abilities stop? You are ultimately constrained only by this view of yourself. Your true potential lies at the edge and just beyond your current belief.
b) Go to an edge once a day, then go beyond – talk to someone new, change your approach, switch roles, change position in a meeting, invoke random!
c) Share your experience with a partner, encourage each other to find new ground.

Your attitude will already have shifted and your ability to choose what it will now become has returned.

49.
SHARPEN
THE AXE

Abraham Lincoln famously said: *"To cut down a tree in five minutes, spend three minutes sharpening your axe."* Similarly, Mahatma Gandhi was quoted as saying that on days when he had most to do, he would get up earlier and meditate longer!

How do you sharpen your axe?

Turning up to your duty every day expecting peak performance every time, without sufficient rest, relaxation, reflection and rejuvenation (sharpening your axe) places unrealistic demands on your automatic attitude selector and your attitude resilience.

The more you progress in your career and personally evolve, the more environmental friction you are likely to attract, compounding further the need for time given to axe-sharpening.

The friction, demands and challenges you attract will increase and will be different too; new versions of old challenges to the way you are, the way you go about things, your habits and how you move forward.

To ensure your attitude continues to soar (or perhaps saw!), it will need sharpening.

● ● ●

● ● ●

a) Read two Attitude Shifters from this book before your working day begins.
b) Write for three minutes about the impact you seek to have today.
c) Insert your own axe-sharpening method here – it may be rest and relaxation based, reading or listing to inspirational material, speaking to mentors and motivators.

Monitor the effectiveness of each of your sharpening techniques, refine or replace them as your experience informs.

"TO CUT DOWN A TREE IN FIVE MINUTES, SPEND THREE MINUTES SHARPENING YOUR AXE."

ABRAHAM LINCOLN

50.
THE ATTITUDE
ADVISOR

Having completed your work on some or all of the Attitude Shifters, you are ready for what is deliberately the ultimate attitude shifter!

It is possible to turn directly to this chapter without working on and embedding any of the previous 49, however, the likelihood of it being your single technique to a new permanent attitude shifting state, or even getting the results that you deeply seek, is low. The more work you have done on the previous chapters, the more effective your results will be with this, the Attitude Advisor.

Picture the scene; you are just about to go into a challenging press conference to deliver a difficult message to an audience of journalists. You know that your mood, attitude and anxieties will affect your performance and alter the way in which the room receives your words. Your body is tense as you concentrate on too many things in the same moment, hopes, intentions, fears, doubts.

Your team of assistants, advisors and private secretaries gather in the waiting room to brief you and help you become calm and centered, ready to select your attitude.

"Today requires you to be humbled and concerned," they advise.

● ● ●

• • •

They suggest and work with you to practise and prepare that attitude; the words; the phrases; the body position; your tone; your
pace; your breathing; etc.

And slowly your mind and body align, because the selected attitude is in your range, it is not unfamiliar or false, your mood shifts,
quiet inner-confidence returns and with it an immense boost to
your resilience, ready to face whatever the pack of news hounds
throw at you.

This will actually happen every day. Consciously work with this
book on a daily basis and observe the advice from your current
colleagues and the (automatic) choices they make.

Work with this metaphor to be like your actual situation. Who is on
your support team? If they don't yet exist, go inside to your own
reference points, take the quiet moment, listen to the sage-like
advice and shift your attitude.

Note: see the **Attitude Selector List** (next page) to inform your
attitude selection.

THE MORE WORK YOU HAVE DONE
ON THE PREVIOUS CHAPTERS,
THE MORE EFFECTIVE YOUR
RESULTS WILL BE WITH THIS,
THE ATTITUDE ADVISOR.

ATTITUDE SELECTOR LIST

Putting a word or words on your attitude can help keep you on course through the day.

Here are my favourites, to which of course you should add your own. Pick the attitudes from the list that you would want to have as part of your everyday life. Work with up to three at a time, for a few days. Don't change them until you feel comfortable and familiar with them.

ACCURATE	CONSIDERED
ALOOF	**COOPERATIVE**
AMBITIOUS	DECISIVE
ASSERTIVE	**DELIBERATE**
ATTENTIVE	DETAILED
BALANCED	**DETERMINED**
BOLD	DEVOTED
BRAVE	**DIPLOMATIC**
CAN DO	DRIVING
CANDID	**EAGER**
CAREFUL	EASY GOING
CARING	**EMPATHIC**
CONFIDENT	ENERGETIC

ENGAGING	OPEN
ENTHUSIASTIC	**PACEY**
EVERYTHING IS OKAY	POLITE
EXACT	**POSITIVE**
FLEXIBLE	PRACTICAL
FOCUSED	**QUIET**
FORCEFUL	RATIONAL
FRANK	**READY FOR ANYTHING**
FRIENDLY	READY TO HELP
GENTLE	**SELFLESS**
GIVING	SENSITIVE
HONEST	**SINCERE**
HELPFUL	SOCIABLE
HUMBLE	**STEADY**
INDEPENDENT	STOIC
INVOLVED	**SUPPORTIVE**
KIND	THOUGHTFUL
LET'S JUST DO IT	**UPBEAT**
LOVING	VERSATILE
LOYAL	**WILLING TO CHANGE**
METHODICAL	YES TO EVERYTHING

REFERENCES AND FURTHER READING

ATTITUDE INSPIRERS

Dr Wayne W Dyer - www.drwaynedyer.com

Mike Dooley – www.tut.com

Jay Perry – www.jayperry.com

Eckhart Tolle - https://www.eckharttolletv.com/p/raq8o5

Archimedes (he of the eureka moment)

Epictetus

BOOKS

The One Minute Manager by Ken Blanchard and Spencer Johnson

The Power of Intention by Wayne Dyer

The Strangest Secret by Earl Nightingale

ABOUT THE AUTHOR

SIMON TYLER

My work with leaders, thinkers and creative entrepreneurs has led me to speak and write about my experience of coaching and mentoring successful men and women to lead and live with simplicity, impact and deliberate positive attitude.

I have been privileged over the years to work with hundreds of talented corporate clients to shift their attitudes and professional practices in a way that transforms their approach to business and causes undeniable measurable change in their personal, as well as commercial, lives. I love cutting through endless complication and frustration, doing my bit to liberate leaders, executives, CEOs, managers and business teams, shifting their attitudes, enhancing their impact and simplifying their way forward.

A few years ago, I worked with Kate Duffy and Joanne Dunleavy in the UK and the USA on the *Attitude Vitamin* project. The seeds of that collaboration have blossomed into *The Attitude Book*.

I have worked with over 1,000 leaders and executives in person and have been hired by many leading and evolving global corporations, to engage with teams and individual leaders. I am glad to have collaborated privately with executives across the world.

My previous books, *The Simple Way*, *The 'Keep It Simple' Book* and *The Impact Book* work in conjunction with this, *The Attitude Book*, to pragmatically inspire personal development. I am deeply passionate about Simplicity, Impact and Attitude and will spend all of my days influencing positive change with them around the world.

CONTACT THE AUTHOR FOR CONFERENCE OR SEMINAR SPEECHES, COACHING, MENTORING AND FACILITATING:

contact@simontyler.com
simontyler.com

in linkedin.com/in/simontyler/
🐦 @simplysimont
📷 @simplysimontyler

ALSO BY THE AUTHOR
* *The Simple Way* – published by Marshall Cavendish
* *The 'Keep It Simple' Book*, *The Impact Code* and *The Impact Book* – published by LID publishing
* *Going Bananas!* – a children's story – self published
* *Simple Notes* – published on the web every two weeks, free subscription at **simontyler.com**.

Sharing knowledge since 1993

- 1993 Madrid
- 2008 Mexico DF and Monterrey
- 2010 London
- 2011 New York and Buenos Aires
- 2012 Bogotá
- 2014 Shanghai